Francis Frith's
THE SOUTH HAMS

PHOTOGRAPHIC MEMORIES

Francis Frith's

THE SOUTH HAMS

◆

Martin Dunning

FRITH
BOOK CO

First published in the United Kingdom in 2000 by
Frith Book Company Ltd

British Library Cataloguing in Publication Data

Francis Frith's The South Hams
Martin Dunning
ISBN 1-85937-220-1

Frith Book Company Ltd
Frith's Barn, Teffont,
Salisbury, Wiltshire SP3 5QP
Tel: +44 (0) 1722 716 376
Email: info@frithbook.co.uk
www.frithbook.co.uk

Printed and bound in Great Britain

Front Cover: Kingsbridge, Fore Street 1896 38429

AS WITH ANY HISTORICAL DATABASE THE FRITH ARCHIVE IS CONSTANTLY BEING CORRECTED AND IMPROVED
AND THE PUBLISHERS WOULD WELCOME INFORMATION ON OMISSIONS OR INACCURACIES

Contents

Francis Frith: *Victorian Pioneer*

FRANCIS FRITH, Victorian founder of the world-famous photographic archive, was a complex and multi-talented man. A devout Quaker and a highly successful Victorian businessman, Frith was both philosophic by nature and pioneering in outlook.

By 1855 Francis Frith had already established a wholesale grocery business in Liverpool, and sold it for the astonishing sum of £200,000, which is the equivalent today of over £15,000,000. Now a multi-millionaire, he was able to indulge his passion for travel. As a child he had pored over travel books written by early explorers, and his fancy and imagination had been stirred by family holidays to the sublime mountain regions of Wales and Scotland. 'What a land of spirit-stirring and enriching scenes and places!' he had written. He was to return to these scenes of grandeur in later years to 'recapture the thousands of vivid and tender memories', but with a different purpose. Now in his thirties, and captivated by the new science of photography, Frith set out on a series of pioneering journeys to the Nile regions that occupied him from 1856 until 1860.

Intrigue and Adventure

He took with him on his travels a specially-designed wicker carriage that acted as both dark-room and sleeping chamber. These far-flung journeys were packed with intrigue and adventure. In his life story, written when he was sixty-three, Frith tells of being held captive by bandits, and of fighting 'an awful midnight battle to the very point of surrender with a deadly pack of hungry, wild dogs'. Sporting flowing Arab costume, Frith arrived at Akaba by camel seventy years before Lawrence, where he encountered 'desert princes and rival sheikhs, blazing with jewel-hilted swords'.

During these extraordinary adventures he was assiduously exploring the desert regions bordering the Nile and patiently recording the antiquities and peoples with his camera. He was the first photographer to venture beyond the sixth cataract. Africa was still the mysterious 'Dark Continent', and Stanley and Livingstone's historic meeting was a decade into the future. The conditions for picture taking confound belief. He laboured for hours in his wicker dark-room in the sweltering heat of the desert, while the volatile chemicals fizzed dangerously in their trays. Often he was forced to work in remote tombs and caves where conditions were cooler. Back in London he exhibited his photographs and was 'rapturously cheered' by members of the Royal Society. His reputation as a photographer was made overnight. An eminent modern historian has likened their impact on the population of the time to that on our own generation of the first photographs taken on the surface of the moon.

Venture of a Life-Time

Characteristically, Frith quickly spotted the opportunity to create a new business as a specialist publisher of photographs. He lived in an era of immense and sometimes violent change. For the poor in the early part of Victoria's reign work was a drudge and the hours long, and people had precious little free time to enjoy themselves. Most had no transport other than a cart or gig at their disposal, and had not travelled far beyond the boundaries of their own town or village.

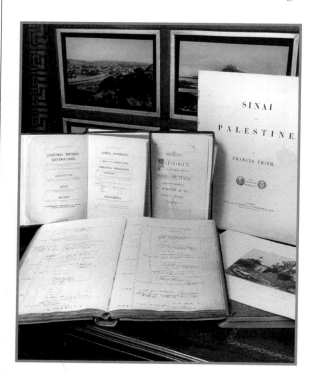

However, by the 1870s, the railways had threaded their way across the country, and Bank Holidays and half-day Saturdays had been made obligatory by Act of Parliament. All of a sudden the ordinary working man and his family were able to enjoy days out and see a little more of the world.

With characteristic business acumen, Francis Frith foresaw that these new tourists would enjoy having souvenirs to commemorate their days out. In 1860 he married Mary Ann Rosling and set out with the intention of photographing every city, town and village in Britain. For the next thirty years he travelled the country by train and by pony and trap, producing fine photographs of seaside resorts and beauty spots that were keenly bought by millions of Victorians. These prints were painstakingly pasted into family albums and pored over during the dark nights of winter, rekindling precious memories of summer excursions.

The Rise of Frith & Co

Frith's studio was soon supplying retail shops all over the country. To meet the demand he gathered about him a small team of photographers, and published the work of independent artist-photographers of the calibre of Roger Fenton and Francis Bedford. In order to gain some understanding of the scale of Frith's business one only has to look at the catalogue issued by Frith & Co in 1886: it runs to some 670 pages, listing not only many thousands of views of the British Isles but also many photographs of most European countries, and China, Japan, the USA and Canada – note the sample page shown above

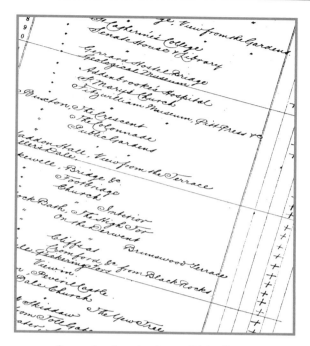

from the hand-written *Frith & Co* ledgers detailing pictures taken. By 1890 Frith had created the greatest specialist photographic publishing company in the world, with over 2,000 outlets – more than the combined number that Boots and WH Smith have today! The picture on the right shows the *Frith & Co* display board at Ingleton in the Yorkshire Dales. Beautifully constructed with mahogany frame and gilt inserts, it could display up to a dozen local scenes.

Postcard Bonanza

The ever-popular holiday postcard we know today took many years to develop. In 1870 the Post Office issued the first plain cards, with a pre-printed stamp on one face. In 1894 they allowed other publishers' cards to be sent through the mail with an attached adhesive halfpenny stamp. Demand grew rapidly, and in 1895 a new size of postcard was permitted

called the court card, but there was little room for illustration. In 1899, a year after Frith's death, a new card measuring 5.5 x 3.5 inches became the standard format, but it was not until 1902 that the divided back came into being, with address and message on one face and a full-size illustration on the other. *Frith & Co* were in the vanguard of postcard development, and Frith's sons Eustace and Cyril continued their father's monumental task, expanding the number of views offered to the public and recording more and more places in Britain, as the coasts and countryside were opened up to mass travel.

Francis Frith died in 1898 at his villa in Cannes, his great project still growing. The archive he created continued in business for another seventy years. By 1970 it contained over a third of a million pictures of 7,000 cities, towns and villages. The massive photographic record Frith has left to us stands as a living monument to a special and very remarkable man.

Frith's Archive: *A Unique Legacy*

FRANCIS FRITH'S legacy to us today is of immense significance and value, for the magnificent archive of evocative photographs he created provides a unique record of change in 7,000 cities, towns and villages throughout Britain over a century and more. Frith and his fellow studio photographers revisited locations many times down the years to update their views, compiling for us an enthralling and colourful pageant of British life and character.

We tend to think of Frith's sepia views of Britain as nostalgic, for most of us use them to conjure up memories of places in our own lives with which we have family associations. It often makes us forget that to Francis Frith they were records of daily life as it was actually being lived in the cities, towns and villages of his day. The Victorian age was one of great and often bewildering change for ordinary people, and though the pictures evoke an impression of slower times, life was as busy and hectic as it is today.

We are fortunate that Frith was a photographer of the people, dedicated to recording the minutiae of everyday life. For it is this sheer wealth of visual data, the painstaking chronicle of changes in dress, transport, street layouts, buildings, housing, engineering and landscape that captivates us so much today. His remarkable images offer us a powerful link with the past and with the lives of our ancestors.

Today's Technology

Computers have now made it possible for Frith's many thousands of images to be accessed almost instantly. In the Frith archive today, each photograph is carefully 'digitised' then stored on a CD Rom. Frith archivists can locate a single photograph amongst thousands within seconds. Views can be catalogued and sorted under a variety of categories of place and content to the immediate benefit of researchers.

Inexpensive reference prints can be created for them at the touch of a mouse button, and a wide range of books and other printed materials assembled and published for a wider, more general readership - in the next twelve months over a hundred Frith local history titles will be published! The day-to-day workings of the archive are very different from how they were in Francis Frith's time: imagine the herculean task of sorting through eleven tons of glass negatives as Frith had to do to locate a

See Frith at www. frithbook.co.uk

particular sequence of pictures! Yet the archive still prides itself on maintaining the same high standards of excellence laid down by Francis Frith, including the painstaking cataloguing and indexing of every view.

It is curious to reflect on how the internet now allows researchers in America and elsewhere greater instant access to the archive than Frith himself ever enjoyed. Many thousands of individual views can be called up on screen within seconds on one of the Frith internet sites, enabling people living continents away to revisit the streets of their ancestral home town, or view places in Britain where they have enjoyed holidays. Many overseas researchers welcome the chance to view special theme selections, such as transport, sports, costume and ancient monuments.

We are certain that Francis Frith would have heartily approved of these modern developments in imaging techniques, for he himself was always working at the very limits of Victorian photographic technology.

The Value of the Archive Today

Because of the benefits brought by the computer, Frith's images are increasingly studied by social historians, by researchers into genealogy and ancestory, by architects, town planners, and by teachers and schoolchildren involved in local history projects.

In addition, the archive offers every one of us an opportunity to examine the places where we and our families have lived and worked down the years. Highly successful in Frith's own era, the archive is now, a century and more on, entering a new phase of popularity.

The Past in Tune with the Future

Historians consider the Francis Frith Collection to be of prime national importance. It is the only archive of its kind remaining in private ownership and has been valued at a million pounds. However, this figure is now rapidly increasing as digital technology enables more and more people around the world to enjoy its benefits.

Francis Frith's archive is now housed in an historic timber barn in the beautiful village of Teffont in Wiltshire. Its founder would not recognize the archive office as it is today. In place of the many thousands of dusty boxes containing glass plate negatives and an all-pervading odour of photographic chemicals, there are now ranks of computer screens. He would be amazed to watch his images travelling round the world at unimaginable speeds through network and internet lines.

The archive's future is both bright and exciting. Francis Frith, with his unshakeable belief in making photographs available to the greatest number of people, would undoubtedly approve of what is being done today with his lifetime's work. His photographs, depicting our shared past, are now bringing pleasure and enlightenment to millions around the world a century and more after his death.

THE SOUTH HAMS - *An Introduction*

THE SOUTH HAMS is an area with a very particular identity. It stretches from Plymouth in the west to Torbay in the east; to the north lie the hills of Dartmoor, and to the south the sea. Within its 343 square miles there are no motorways or dual carriageways, and the A379, which runs east to west through the South Devon countryside, is not an A-road in the sense that many might understand it - in places it is sufficiently narrow to require traffic to pull in to let oncoming vehicles pass, and if you decide to travel from Plymouth to Dartmouth and back, a round trip of 72 miles, then you may as well set aside the whole day in which to do it.

Off the main roads, things slow down even further. Narrow lanes wind between the characteristic high Devon hedges, and the ability to reverse perhaps two hundred yards to the nearest gateway to allow a tractor towing a trailer-load of hay to squeeze past is essential. Local cars are easily distinguished from those of visitors by taking a peek at the nearside paintwork: it will be dulled by a mass of small scratches from the bramble, blackthorn and hazel of the hedges. In short, the landscape of the South Hams was not made for the motor car.

Although little of the area is actually moorland, the bleak hills of Dartmoor are responsible in no short measure for the landscape. Dartmoor receives 70 or 80 inches of rain annually (Plymouth gets just 30), and all that water has to go somewhere. Over the millennia, water rushing down off the high plateau of the moors has carved deep, snaking valleys; when the sea level rose at the end of the last Ice Age, these became flooded far inland, giving rise to the tidal estuaries with

their mudflats and creeks which are such an important part of the South Hams.

The major rivers of the area are relatively short - even the Dart is less then fifty miles long - but they cut through the coastal plain every few miles, dividing the area into neat little packets and forming simultaneously a barrier to and medium for travel. All flow north to south and exhibit, in their short length, the classic stages of a river's life that we remember from GCSE geography: the young river, babbling its way exuberantly down rapids and cascades as it runs down off the hills; the mature river, ambling thoughtfully through fields and wooded hills; and the old river, looping sedately over its flood plain before spilling into the tidal estuary.

The Plym, Yealm, Erme and Avon, the Kingsbridge River and the Dart - all these have their own character, and all have played their part in the history of the South Hams. Until a few centuries ago they were an important source of food. Salmon and bass from the estuaries, shellfish from the mudflats, pike, perch and rudd from the flat waters of Slapton Ley, and wildfowl from the marshes and woods would all have been staples.

Settlements grew up around fords, for it was here that people crossed paths, made contacts and traded; eventually, when the hamlet or village had become bustling and wealthy enough to warrant and afford it, a bridge was built. Thus the old tidal ford at Aveton Gifford was in time spanned by the bridge that today carries the A379, while at places such as Harbertonford, the ford and the bridge can still be seen side by side.

The coast has been settled for thousands of years. As in Cornwall, early man saw an opportunity for security in the mighty natural citadels of headlands such as the Bolt, and made his home there. An Iron Age fortress can still be seen at Bolt Tail, while at other less obvious sites such as Slapton, smaller hills sprouted earthworks behind which the occupants could shelter in times of trouble. Those living by the sea also made their living from the sea. Bigbury Bay was a noted pilchard fishery, commemorated in the name of the inn on Burgh Island; and from the great shingle bank which forms the shore of Start Bay fishermen dragged their little boats down the beach and went to sea in search of whiting, mackerel, herring, mullet and shellfish. Every estuary and every cove had its own fleet, from the crabbers of Newton Ferrers on the Yealm to the salmon men of the Avon and the Dart.

In the hinterland north of the cliffs and between the rivers lies the farmland. It is a patchwork of fields like no other patchwork in Britain; vibrantly green from the ample rainfall and warm climate, the fields of the South Hams draw their nourishment from rich red soils. The

contrasting green and red fields, set on a wrinkled, folded landscape with thick woodlands in the valleys and isolated copses capping the higher hills, are what gives the area its beauty - and what gave it its wealth.

As far back as Norman times the South Hams was recognised as a rich farming area. William the Conqueror, after his conquest in 1066, rewarded his nobles and knights with estates and manors. Land in Devon, closer to home for the Normans and their Breton allies, was much in demand; by the time of the Domesday book in 1086, many manors were in the hands of Norman landlords. Ralf de Feugeres held Galmpton, Walter of Douai Stoke Fleming, and the Breton Judhael leased the valuable waterside estate of Stoke Gabriel from the king.

The Domesday book lists numbers of villagers, names of landlords, notable premises such as watermills, and livestock. The figures for livestock are particularly revealing: while most manors are recorded as having a few pigs and cattle, almost every one has at least a hundred sheep, and in some cases, such as Buckfast, over 600. Wool was to be the making of many a rich merchant. The soft, pure water of the rivers provided the power, and mills sprang up everywhere. Totnes, Ashburton, Buckfastleigh, Modbury - all grew wealthy producing cloth. Like any commodity, there was a regular cycle of boom and bust, but as

late as the 19th century fortunes were being made until the rise of the Yorkshire woollen industry sounded the death knell for the fullers and weavers of the South Hams.

Further down the rivers, ports at the mouth of the sheltered estuaries began to flourish. There had always been a lively trade up and down these highways - coal, cattle, grain, potatoes and livestock were traded at market towns on the rivers - but the wool trade gave development a new impetus. John Hawley - who combined being a merchant with another life as privateer and raider of French ports - built the first castle at Dartmouth in the 13th century to protect his business interests. As the ports of the South Hams grew, more ships called to trade or to be provisioned or merely to take a breather before setting out on long ocean passages. The Pilgrim Fathers stopped off for repairs at Dartmouth before their historic voyage to the new world, fishing fleets sailed to work the Grand Banks off Newfoundland, and the Salcombe Clippers traded far and wide.

While Salcombe and Dartmouth, with their deep, sheltered anchorages serviced by hundreds of boatyards, chandlers, blacksmiths and sailmakers, were the hub of the growing international trade, coastal trade carried on as it had done for centuries. Limestone from Plymouth was carried to provide roadstone and lime, coasters shipped cargoes into barges at

Bantham for transport up the Avon, and people travelled the rivers in preference to the roads to buy and sell anything that could be traded. Lookouts on the cliffs watched for invaders such as the Spanish Armada or Bonaparte, and also for incoming shipping. The Lloyds' lookout high on Bolt Head was part of a chain of signal stations which alerted merchants and shipowners in London of the impending arrival of a ship carrying, say, tea, often setting off a frenzy of speculation on the markets.

Through all the ups and downs of trade and war, the farmers farmed, the fishermen fished and the smugglers sneaked around avoiding the revenue men. Wooden ships gave way to iron, and the arrival of the railways - to Totnes and Yealmpton, via Torquay to Kingswear opposite Dartmouth, and down the beautiful 'Primrose Line' from South Brent to Kingsbridge - offered new opportunities. Soon coal was being hauled inland to the gasworks at Torquay; of more lasting importance, the tourists and day trippers began to arrive. Both Dartmouth and Salcombe became fashionable places, frequented by the wealthy with their private yachts and from time to time graced by a royal presence.

Two World Wars passed, each causing its own type of disruption. In the First War the enlisting of men to fight in the trenches left the land short of labourers, and a huge sale of horses to the War Ministry (which took place on Kingsbridge Quay) resulted in a shortage of animals to work the land and probably speeded up the introduction of the tractor. The Second World War saw the estuaries of Dartmouth and Salcombe crammed with Allied ships and landing craft, Bolt Head's breezy plateau turned into an airfield and 3,000 people evacuated from the shores of Start Bay to allow US forces to rehearse the Normandy landings.

In recent years change has continued. The branch railways closed - the Primrose Line in 1963 and the Kingswear line in 1969 - and marinas and pleasure craft replaced the coasters, freighters and fishing boats. Tourist attractions such as Woodlands Leisure Park and the Shire Horse Centre have appeared, and villages like Ivybridge have grown out of all recognition.

Although it might sometimes seem that every barn in the South Hams has been converted (albeit tastefully) to house the growing throng of urban professionals, the patchwork of fields remains, dotted with sheep and the deep red South Devon cattle. And take a walk over Bolt Head on a breezy day, or nip down to a little creek like Batson on the Dart or Cofflete on the Yealm, and it will not seem all that different from the way it looked when William was handing out estates to his conquering Normans.

The Plym

SHAUGH PRIOR
SHAUGH BRIDGE c1876 8316
Shaugh Bridge lies a few yards downstream of the confluence of the Meavy and the Plym. The Plym, flowing under the bridge on its way to the sea at Plymouth, used to run white with run-off from the clay tips upstream.

SHAUGH PRIOR, THE DEWERSTONE c1960 S356001

SHAUGH PRIOR
The Dewerstone c1960
This little outcrop is on the hill top above the Dewerstone itself - a magnificent 170ft granite sentinel which rises from the steep, wooded hillside above the Plym. The name is a reference to the devil, who is supposed to ride across the cliffs in the dead of night - hence one of the buttresses being named Devil's Rock.

◆

SHAUGH PRIOR
The Village c1965
The village has grown considerably since this picture was taken, and now extends a good half mile down the hill to the left. The white building on the left is the White Thorn Inn, and on the far right is the school. In the background is West Down.

SHAUGH PRIOR, THE VILLAGE c1965 S356018

WOTTER
The Moorland Hotel c1960
It has to be said that the Moorland Hotel is not one of Dartmoor's architectural gems. However, it is well-appointed, and it occupies a superb site just on the edge of the moor. It was built in 1930.

WOTTER
The China Clay Pits c1960
The clay workings of Lee Moor provide a lot of employment, but they are also something of a blot on the landscape and are visible from ten miles out to sea. In the background are Penn Beacon and Shell Top; the latter is one of the highest points on the south moor at over 1,500 feet.

WOTTER, THE MOORLAND HOTEL c1960   W277003

WOTTER, THE CHINA CLAY PITS c1960   W277004

WOTTER, A VIEW FROM THE MOORS c1960 W277006

From Wotter, on a clear day, one can see the deep, wooded valley of the River Yealm snaking its way southwards to the sea. On the left is the Methodist Chapel, and the terrace on the right was built to house clay workers.

PLYMPTON, ST MAURICE 1890 22503

Probably taken from Dorsmouth Rock to the south-east, this photograph shows just how compact Plympton used to be; the dark ridge immediately behind the village is now a vast housing estate. In the distance (centre) is Hemerdon Ball, once the site of the only tungsten mine in the country.

PLYMPTON, ST MARY 1898 41939

This is another picture which shows how much things have changed. Most of the fields in the middle distance are now occupied by the middle-class suburb of Woodford. The terraces in front of the church were once the home of the monks, who used the back entrance to the church to avoid contact with the less-than-holy locals.

PLYMPTON, THE RAILWAY STATION 1898 41942

The station closed in 1959, but the line still carries trains between Paddington and Penzance. In the background is Colebrook, where the Victorian houses are unchanged today, and in the foreground is the Tory Brook, which eventually joins the Plym at Marsh Mills. The rough lane is now a broad road carrying commuters from Chaddlewood.

PLYMPTON, ST MARY
FORE STREET 1898 41944
There are some businesses here that
have long faded away - J Dart, Saddler
and Boot Depot (left) and White's
Smithing Forge - but also some that are
still going. The Western Morning News
(advertised outside Parish's on the left)
is still the local paper, and to the right
of the doorway is a display of Frith's
photographs.

PLYMSTOCK, RADFORD PARK TEA HOUSES c1876 8336

This was the author's childhood playground. Radford Pond adjoins Hooe Lake, a tidal offshoot of the Plym. The buildings were part of the long-defunct Radford estate, and have long since fallen into ruin. On the right is the boathouse, while the building on the left, so local legend says, is where Sir Francis Drake used to entertain his mistresses.

The Yealm

YEALMPTON
A Thatched Cottage c1950 Y9001
This charming cottage by the side of the A379 is now a
restaurant called Mother Hubbard's Cottage. The original
nursery rhyme, written by Sarah Martin in 1805, was based on
the housekeeper on the nearby Kitley estate.

NEWTON FERRERS, THE RIVER YEALM 1890 22486
The twin villages of Newton Ferrers (left) and Noss Mayo (right) lie on either side of the estuary of the Yealm. The age-old rivalry between them is traditionally ascribed to the fact that Newton was originally Anglo-Saxon, while Noss claims an older lineage as a Celtic settlement.

NEWTON FERRERS, THE RIVER YEALM 1890 22492
This view was taken from Noss, looking across the river. Newton Ferrers takes its name from Henry de Ferrers, a rich Norman mine-owner, who fought with William the Conqueror and was rewarded with 200 manors, including Bere Ferrers on the Tavy and Churston Ferrers near Torquay.

NOSS MAYO, WATERSIDE SCENE c1950 N49054
Newton and Noss once supported a thriving fishing fleet - at the turn of the 19th century as many as 30 crabbers would be working. The fleet has declined now, but replica crabbers are still raced in the Yealm regatta every August.

NOSS MAYO, POINT HOUSE AND THE GLOBE INN FROM NOSS HARD c1950 N49056
The Globe still stands on the very edge of the creek; today it is known as the Ship, and is much extended and altered. Around it, however, Noss remains unchanged.

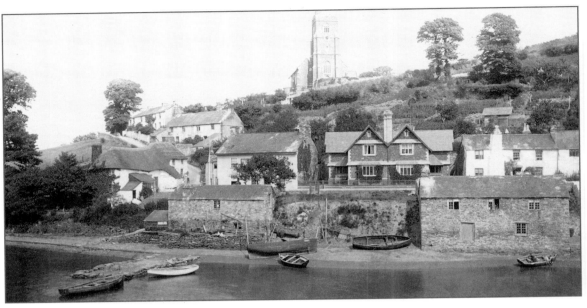

NOSS MAYO, THE RIVER YEALM 1890 22490

The church of St Peter had not long been completed when this picture was taken. The foundation was laid in 1880 by Mrs Edward Baring, whose husband became Lord Revelstoke in 1885. A member of the well-known banking family, Lord Revelstoke lived at nearby Membland Hall, where visitors included Edward VII, Czar Nicholas, the Rothschilds and William Gladstone.

NOSS MAYO, THE SWAN INN AND THE HILL c1950 N49061

The lovely thatched cottage from photograph No 22490 has gone, and has been replaced by the Post Office. The Swan Inn is still there, and remains in business to this day. The steep little hill is no place to suffer brake problems, believe me!

NOSS MAYO, THE RIVER 1931 83980
The promontory that runs from the pool out and round to Stoke Beach belonged in the 13th century to Matthieu Fitz Herbert and was known as La Nasse de Matthieu, a name which in time became corrupted to Noss Mayo.

NOSS MAYO, THE HARBOUR c1960 N49026
At low tide it is possible to walk from Noss to Newton across the little causeway known as the Voss, which lands below the Dolphin Inn (dead centre, just above the building with the dark doorway in its gable end). Above the trees rises the tower of the Church of the Holy Cross - minus its pinnacles, which were destroyed by lightning in 1946.

NOSS MAYO
GENERAL VIEW 1931 83978
The coach is parked outside the Tilley Institute, built in 1878 and still in use as a snooker and billiards room. To its left is the village hall, built in 1839. On the far left is the Methodist Chapel, built in 1870.

NOSS MAYO, STOKE BEACH c1960 N49011

The tents have long gone, to be replaced today by a large caravan site. On the right, Burgh Island is just visible across Bigbury Bay. The clifftop on the left is the site of the nine-mile ride, a carriage track laid by Lord Revelstoke which follows the clifftop from Hilsea Point round the Warren at the mouth of the Yealm.

WEMBURY, THE SWIMMING POOL, WEMBURY POINT HOLIDAY CAMP c1950 W604003

Heybrook Bay Lido, consisting of 200 wooden chalets, operated up to World War Two, and the pool survived a little longer. Today the remains of the pool can still be seen. The hillside behind is home to the Royal Navy's gunnery school, HMS Cambridge, which is due to close in 2001.

WEMBURY, THE CHURCH AND THE BEACH c1955 W604002
A church has existed here since a Saxon oratory was built in the 10th century. The present church, St Werburgh's, dates from the 14th century. In the background is the mouth of the River Yealm, and to its right is the Warren, round which runs the nine-mile drive.

HEYBROOK BAY, THE COAST ROAD c1955 H241005
The village is now considerably larger; the entire hillside was built up in the fifties and sixties. The large building in the centre is now the Eddystone Inn, which today has a fine terrace with views (on a clear day) over the English Channel to the Eddystone Lighthouse.

The Erme

HARFORD
THE CHURCH c1955 H237005
This 15th-century church contains the tomb of Thomas Williams, Speaker of the House of Commons in 1536, and also the tomb of the parents of John Prideaux, Bishop of Worcester from 1641-50. In the background are the Lee Moor clay workings.

HARFORD, THE BRIDGE C1955 H237006

This old packhorse bridge spans the Erme, reputedly one of the fastest-flowing rivers in the country. It rises at Erme Head, 1,300 feet up on the moors and eight miles north of Harford. A mile upstream from Harford is Piles Copse, a woodland of stunted oaks which is one of the last remnants of the forest which once covered much of the moor.

HARFORD
The Ancient Cross and the Moors c1960
This granite cross in Harford churchyard was once used as a gatepost - a fate not uncommon for these handy-sized pieces of stone. In the background is Hanger Down with, on the left, Hanger Down Clump, a popular trysting-spot for locals.

HARFORD
The Mill 1886
In 1549 one John Bury, owner of a tin mill hereabouts, led the Prayer Book Rebellion against the introduction of Thomas Cranmer's Book of Common Prayer, the first to be published in English rather than Latin. The rebellion fizzled out, and Bury was hung in 1550.

HARFORD, THE ANCIENT CROSS AND THE MOORS c1960 H237022

HARFORD, THE MILL 1886 19105

IVYBRIDGE, THE BRIDGE c1876   8306

IVYBRIDGE
The Bridge c1876
There are records of a packhorse bridge here going back to 1280. The present bridge was built in about 1826, and is wider than its predecessors to allow the passage of stage coaches. Included in the structure are boundary stones: these have a dual role, for they also act as 'kicking stones' to protect the parapet.

◆

IVYBRIDGE
The Bridge c1876
Just upstream of the bridge on the east bank was the London Hotel, a much-loved hostelry which was once the centre of social life in the town. Built in the late 18th century, it was known as Mallet's Hotel in the 19th century. It closed in 1991; the premises were bought by South Hams District Council and converted to offices and flats.

IVYBRIDGE, THE BRIDGE c1876   8307

IVYBRIDGE, ALLEN'S PAPER MILL c1876 8310

The original water-powered mill was built here in the late 18th century. It burned down on 5 May 1914, but was rebuilt, and produced paper for the old white five pound notes and for stamps. The present mill is owned by Arjo Wiggins.

IVYBRIDGE, FORE STREET c1955 122018

Fore Street was built around 1830. The King's Arms Hotel (in the background) became the Fighting Cocks, and is now the Exchange. The house behind the sign for the fish and chip shop was once the home of the famous Dartmoor writer William Crossing.

IVYBRIDGE, THE CHURCH c1876 8305

Although it was a thriving village for several centuries, Ivybridge did not have its own church until 1802. The new church of St John was built in 1882, and the parish of Ivybridge was created in 1892 from parts of the parishes of Ugborough and Ermington. The old church (the one in this picture) was bought for £5 in 1925 by Mr H Blight and demolished. The stone was used for houses.

IVYBRIDGE, GENERAL VIEW c1876 8303

Today the population of Ivybridge is nearing 20,000 - a far cry from the 19th century, when the inhabitants numbered perhaps 500. In the background are (from right) Western Beacon, Butterdon Hill, and Glasscombe Ball.

MODBURY, BROAD STREET c1950 M172016

Originally a Saxon settlement ('Moot Burgh'), this delightful little town received its charter and market in 1155 when the population was 400. In the 18th and 19th centuries, the town became very wealthy from the making of woollen serge, and its fine Georgian and Regency houses date from this time.

MODBURY, BROAD STREET c1950 M172012

In its heyday, Modbury had ten pubs and a population of over 2,000, and the annual St George's Fair lasted nine days. With the rise of the Yorkshire woollen industry in the late 19th century, Modbury could no longer compete; by 1960 the population had declined to just over 1,000.

The Avon

SOUTH BRENT, THE STEPPING STONES AND THE VICARAGE C1890 S360504
There was a Christian church in South Brent as far back as the 6th century, and in the 11th century the Manor of Brent (from the Old English 'brant', meaning steep hill) belonged to Buckfast Abbey. The present church of St Petroc was built in 1436, and this old vicarage is now a private house.

SOUTH BRENT
Lydia Bridge c1890
The plaque on the parapet reads: 'Take notice that this bridge (which is a county bridge) is insufficient to carry weights beyond the ordinary traffic of the district and that owners drivers and persons in charge of locomotives are warned against attempting the passage of the bridge without the consent of the County Surveyor. By order of the County Justices'.

◆

GARA BRIDGE
The Railway Station 1896
This station, in the valley of the Avon between South Brent and Loddiswell, was on the Kingsbridge branch line; this was known as the 'Primrose Line', and was reckoned to be the most beautiful line in the country. In its twelve miles it had 48 bridges and a tunnel. It ran from 1893 to 1963.

SOUTH BRENT, LYDIA BRIDGE c1890 S360503

GARA BRIDGE, THE RAILWAY STATION 1896 38434

LODDISWELL, THE OLD SCHOOL HOUSE AND THE VILLAGE c1960 L531014
The village's most famous son was Richard Peek, who was known as 'Little Dick Whittington' after he walked to London to seek his fortune. He became a successful tea broker, was made Sherriff of London, and in 1830 built the nearby Hazelwood House.

LODDISWELL, THE CHURCH 1890 25267
The 14th-century church of St Michael was enlarged in the 15th century, and has a fine Norman font. The north transept was the Woolston Chapel, named after the 17th-century Woolston Manor, home of the Furlong family and later of the Wises.

WOODLEIGH
The Church Gate and the Cottages 1890 25269
The church of St Mary was built in the 14th century and was restored in 1891. One of the few original features to survive was the Easter Sepulchre made by Thomas Smyth, who was rector from 1492 to 1527. The right-hand thatched cottage was the shop and Post Office.

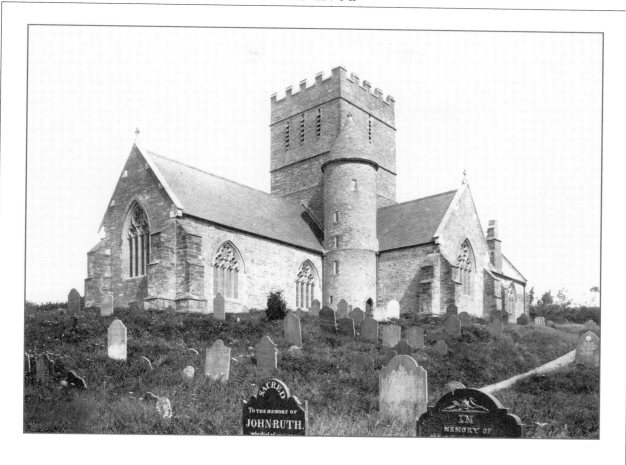

AVETON GIFFORD
The Church from the South-West 1890 24533
One of the oldest churches in Devon, St Andrew's
was built in the late 13th century. It was destroyed by
an air raid in the afternoon of 25 January 1943.
Rebuilding was completed in 1957, and the church
was rededicated in 1970.

BANTHAM, BURGH ISLAND 1904 52458

From the sea, Burgh Island can be mistaken for Rame Head or Looe Island, which both lie to the west. This led in times past to some notable shipwrecks, notably that of HMS Ramillies: in 1760, thinking that she was heading into Plymouth Sound, she was wrecked on Bolt Tail with the loss of 708 of her 734 crew.

BIGBURY-ON-SEA, GENERAL VIEW 1925 78329

At low tide, Burgh Island is linked to the mainland by a broad spit of sand. The tiny building at the top of the Island is a huers' hut, used as a lookout for the vast shoals of pilchards that were once the staple diet of local people, and that were also used to fertilise the fields.

BIGBURY-ON-SEA
Foxhounds on The Beach 1924

The Pilchard Inn - one of the best pubs on the south coast - was built in the 14th century by monks. It was later used by smugglers, including Tom Crocker, who gave his name to the pub opposite on the mainland and was shot dead at the Pilchard. His ghost still haunts the premises.

BIGBURY-ON-SEA
The Burgh Island Hotel 1931

This wonderful art deco hotel was built in 1929 by Archibald Nettlefold, founder of the engineering group GKN. Agatha Christie wrote 'Evil Under the Sun' and 'Then There Were None' here, and other visitors included the Duke of Windsor and the Beatles. The ungainly-looking vehicle is the tractor which is used to get to the island at high tide.

BIGBURY-ON-SEA, FOXHOUNDS ON THE BEACH 1924 76566

BIGBURY-ON-SEA, THE BURGH ISLAND HOTEL 1931 83969

BIGBURY-ON-SEA, BURGH ISLAND CAVE 1925 78339
The Devonian purple and green slates which make up this part of the coast can erode into all sorts of odd shapes.
They are also very reflective: the cliffs near Challaborough, on the western side of Bigbury Bay, sometimes appear to
shimmer silver in bright sunlight.

BIGBURY-ON-SEA, THE VILLAGE 1938 88608

Bigbury-on-Sea is a relatively recent settlement, built in around 1910 as a speculative venture. Many of the original wooden chalets were bought as second homes by Plymouth doctors, who let them out to convalescent patients whom they thought would benefit from the sea air.

RINGMORE, THE CHURCH c1960 R258015

All Saints Church was built in the 13th century on the site of an earlier church. The parish must have been relatively wealthy, for just before World War One it is recorded that the Rectory (now part of a farm) had eight servants, two gardeners and a handyman.

RINGMORE
The Village c1960
This is Hill Cottage, which is still standing and today clad with climbing roses and clematis. To do a 'square' of thatch (10ft by 10ft) requires 420 pounds of reed - it is hard work for the thatcher's mate to bring it up the ladder. The small thatched porch is known as a checkett.

◆

RINGMORE
The Post Office c1960
The Post Office (now closed) occupied at least five different houses; this one is now called Ivy Cottage. The pub down the road used to be called the New Inn, but it changed its name to the Journey's End in honour of R C Sherriff, who wrote his novel of the same name there.

RINGMORE, THE VILLAGE c1960 R258010

RINGMORE, THE POST OFFICE c1960 R258018

BANTHAM, THE RIVER AVON 1924 76567

The estuary of the Avon wiggles its way inland four miles from Bantham. At low tide it is possible to follow a tidal lane, marked by posts, all the way up the western bank to Aveton Gifford. Careful consultation of tide tables is a must!

BANTHAM, THE RIVER AVON c1950 B16002

Sheltered by dunes and a sandy promontory, Bantham provides a safe anchorage, although negotiating the mouth of the river in anything less than perfect conditions can be tricky. The currents are treacherous, and Bantham Beach itself is renowned for its surf.

BANTHAM, THE LANDING PLACE c1950 B16010
Jenkins Yard was the centre of activity when Bantham was a flourishing little port. Small coasters would anchor and offload limestone and coal, which was then taken upriver by barge and sloop. Corn and potatoes were exported.

BANTHAM, THE SLOOP INN 1924 76569
Built in the 16th century, the Sloop was once owned by John Weddon and Nat Claverly, notorious smugglers of rum and brandy. Today it is frequented by day trippers who come to enjoy Bantham's fine beach.

WEST BUCKLAND
The Village 1920 69843
Just behind the small boy is Tidley Cottage, built in
the 17th century: it was one of the smallest cottages
in Devon, measuring just 15ft by 10ft 9in. The
occupants had to climb a ladder to reach the
bedroom through the window, and upstairs there
was no room to stand up. It burned down in 1959,
and the site is now taken by a garage.

The Bolt

THURLESTONE
VIEW FROM THE HOTEL 1925 78315
The offshore pinnacle of Thurlestone Rock has been pierced ('thirled') by the sea, and legend says that on a stormy day the noise of the waves around the rock can be heard five miles away in Kingsbridge. In the background is Bolt Tail.

General View 1930
During the Civil War, the rector of the 13th-century church of All Saints was John Snell, who was chaplain to King Charles. He returned to Thurlestone after the war, but was hounded out by the locals. In the foreground is the Club House of the golf course.

THURLESTONE
The Links 1924
The golf course was started in 1897 by four men: the architect T W Latham, the brewer H G Prowse, A B Crispen, and Dr E A S Elliott. In 1974 Harry Pratt became world-famous when he scored a hole in one at the sixth aged just seven.

THURLESTONE, GENERAL VIEW 1930 83280

THURLESTONE, THE LINKS 1924 76554

THURLESTONE, A THATCHED COTTAGE c1950 T42012

' ... a little artistic taste has been employed even in the thatching, so that they have a difference from that of the same class of cottages in the inland towns of the midland counties'. So wrote Marianne Farningham in the 'Christian World' in Victorian times, but I suspect the inhabitants were more concerned with keeping the weather out than with artistic taste.

SOUTH MILTON, GENERAL VIEW 1927 79892

South Milton lies at the head of the little stream which flows down to Thurlestone, and indeed the beach on which the rock stands is called South Milton Sands. The 14th-century church is another dedicated to All Saints - presumably a ruse by which parishioners could be sure of protection on a wider scale than if the church were dedicated to only one saint.

SOUTH MILTON, THE VILLAGE 1927 79891

A major local trade was that of limestone draying. Limestone was brought from Plymouth by barge and unloaded into Goosey Pool and New Way Gut at South Milton Sands. At low tide, horses pulled drays into the water and the stone was taken inland to be broken and used for roadstone.

SOUTH MILTON, THE VILLAGE 1927 79894

In the 19th and early 20th centuries South Milton's population was largely made up of one family - the Steers. Perhaps this old man is one of that same family.

SOUTH MILTON
Old Houses 1927

South Milton was the home of the last commercial horse-drawn carriage in the South Hams, which operated between the village and Kingsbridge. It ceased to operate in 1977 when Jim Johns died. One of these houses was the Police cottage.

◆

GALMPTON
The Village 1927

In 1086 Galmpton was owned by the Norman Ralf de Feugeres, who paid the King £7 10s annually for the privilege. The fourteen villagers of the time tended 100 sheep - perhaps these animals are their descendants.

SOUTH MILTON, OLD HOUSES 1927 79895

GALMPTON, THE VILLAGE 1927 79898

GALMPTON, THE VILLAGE 1927 79897

GALMPTON
The Village 1927
This is a classic example of the picture-postcard idea of what an English village should be - a thatched cottage with roses round the door and happy children playing on the lawn. However, it was not all idyllic - villages such as this did not even have mains water when this picture was taken.

◆

MALBOROUGH
All Saints' Church 1927
The second most southerly parish in Devon, Malborough occupies a breezy site 400 feet up on the plateau of the Bolt. The tower of the 15th-century church of All Saints, visible from many miles out to sea, is an important navigational feature.

MALBOROUGH, ALL SAINTS' CHURCH 1927 79907

MALBOROUGH
Higher Town 1927 79904
Malborough has the distinction of
having the largest church hall in the
South Hams, which is used by people
and organisations from far and wide. It
was built on the village playing fields
after World War Two.

MALBOROUGH, THE VILLAGE AND THE CHURCH 1890 25262

MALBOROUGH
The Village and the Church 1890
All Saints was re-opened after restoration in 1870: ' ... the opening services were attended by large congregations, all the seats were occupied and many had to stand - a large marquee was erected and some hundreds of people sat down to lunch'.

◆

HOPE COVE
A Coast Scene 1890
'This unusually quiet little cove sometimes presents a curious spectacle, from its being a sheltered retreat for wind-bound vessels, which occasionally lie there for a week, or more, at least, until the breeze is a favourable one'. Thus wrote Mr S P Fox of Kingsbridge in 1874.

HOPE COVE, A COAST SCENE 1890 23063

HOPE COVE, THE VILLAGE AND THE COVE 1935 86952
In 1878, in thanks for the delivery of one of the royal princes from typhoid, the Grand Lodge of Freemasons established a lifeboat at Hope Cove. It was named the 'Alexandra', after the Princess of Wales, as were its three successors. The station closed in 1930 when a more powerful boat was stationed at Salcombe.

HOPE COVE, COTTAGES 1890 25259
These 17th- and 18th-century cottages were once used by the smugglers who ran silk, tobacco and brandy. Apparently there used to be underground passages here, which have now collapsed; they were used to get smugglers out of the village to the sea.

HOPE COVE, THE HARBOUR AND THE BEACH C1950 H112016
Only a few years before this picture was taken, Hope Cove bustled with RAF personnel stationed at the Ground Control Interceptor Station of RAF Hope Cove, a secret radar station which controlled the Spitfires, Typhoons and Mosquitoes which flew from RAF Bolt Head in World War Two.

BOLT HEAD, SOAR MILL COVE 1927 79914
The cove was the scene of one of the last wrecks of a sailing ship on the British coast - that of the three-masted Finnish barque the 'Herzogen Cecilie' in 1936. Local farmers made a small fortune charging the thousands of people who came to gaze at the wreck, just offshore on the Ham Stone.

Kingsbridge and Salcombe

SHERFORD
The Church 1890 25271
The church of St Martin was built in the 14th century from Charlton
slate. The tower is a 15th-century addition, as are the windows. Judging
from the state of the roof in this picture, it would appear to have had
little maintenance in the intervening years.

SHERFORD, THE CHURCH AND THE STREET 1890 25272
Not far from Sherford is the Tudor manor house (now a farm) of Keynedon, once home to the Hals family, who must have been something of a force to be reckoned with - in the 15th century one became a judge and another a bishop.

KINGSBRIDGE, GENERAL VIEW 1924 76511
The first bridge here, originally referred to in a charter of 962, linked two royal estates at Alvington and Chillington, and was therefore known as the 'King's Bridge'. In 1219 the town was granted a market by the Abbot of Buckfastleigh, and in 1258 it became a borough.

KINGSBRIDGE, FORE STREET AND THE GRAMMAR SCHOOL 1895 35626

KINGSBRIDGE
Fore Street and the Grammar School 1895
The school was founded in 1671 by Thomas Crispin, a wealthy fuller in the wool trade. The new Grammar School opened in Kingsley Road in 1931, and the old building now houses the Cookworthy Museum. The oak panelling inside still bears the carved names of the original schoolboys.

◆

KINGSBRIDGE
Fore Street and Shambles 1896
The building with the clock tower was once the Town Hall, but now it houses the Reel Cinema. The clock had only three faces; the one facing away from the road was left blank - it overlooked the workhouse, and the authorities did not want the inmates knowing the time!

KINGSBRIDGE, FORE STREET AND SHAMBLES 1896 38508

KINGSBRIDGE

FORE STREET 1896 38429

The owners of Pound's Temperance Hotel (right) would certainly not have approved of 'white ale', a ferociously powerful local concoction brewed from malt, hops, eggs, flour and a mystery ingredient called 'grout', and which was being served in the Plymouth Inn (see picture No 38429) in the late 19th century.

KINGSBRIDGE, THE MARKET HOUSE AND THE SHAMBLES 1890 24522
This was the commercial centre of the town, with meat and corn markets. The street was once much wider; in 1864 S P Fox wrote of shopkeepers having stalls on the pavement in front of their premises. Eventually these stalls were incorporated into the body of the shop, and the street thus grew narrower.

KINGSBRIDGE, THE RIVER 1924 76516
Kingsbridge was once an important inland port, shipping all manner of cargoes from the quay (right). This end of the creek is now filled in and occupied by an open space with a new bandstand. The Anchor Hotel is now the Quay, and the gabled building between the two garages now houses Boots.

KINGSBRIDGE
General View 1931

On the left is Square's Quay, the last to be reclaimed from the mudflats which once surrounded the town, and the site of a thriving timber yard and sawmill. The church on the skyline is that of St Edmund the Martyr, which stands next to the Market House. The steps on the right were used by steamers such as the 'Kingsbridge Packet' and the 'Queen'.

◆

KINGSBRIDGE
The Esplanade 1896

Kingsbridge's status as the 'capital' of the South Hams, along with its importance as a market centre for the rich farmlands nearby, meant that the wealthy built their town houses here. A steamer is moored on the right, and in the distance the tranquil estuary snakes off towards the sea some six miles away.

KINGSBRIDGE, GENERAL VIEW 1931 83936

KINGSBRIDGE, THE ESPLANADE 1896 38426

KINGSBRIDGE, WESTERN BACK WAY 1924 76524
Fore Street has many little alleyways leading off its steep hill. Western Back Way has an eastern counterpart on the other side of the street. The hillside beyond is now built up.

SALCOMBE, FROM PORTLEMOUTH 1920 69814

Salcombe is Devon's most southerly town. Its population of 2,000 doubles in summer, swelled by visiting yachtsmen. Today's sailors are almost exclusively here for pleasure, a very different state of affairs from the days when half the town were sailors, and when boatyards, sailmakers, blacksmiths and chandlers flourished.

SALCOMBE, THE ROCKSIDE BOATHOUSE 1928 81013A

The famous Salcombe Clippers, of 100-500 tons, were very fast and traded perishable commodities such as oranges and pineapples from the Azores and tobacco, coffee, ginger, sugar and cotton from the West Indies.

EAST PORTLEMOUTH, GENERAL VIEW 1925 78399
Here we have a good view of the Kingsbridge estuary winding inland between the patchwork of fields that is so characteristic of the South Hams. In 1925 there were relatively few boats on the river; today its sheltered waters are home to thousands of pleasure craft.

EAST PORTLEMOUTH, THE VILLAGE 1925 78397
To get from Salcombe to East Portlemouth is ten minutes by ferry - or seventeen miles by road. Running eastwards from here is some of Devon's most spectacular coastline, culminating in Prawle Point, the county's most southerly headland.

The Dart

HOLNE
A Cottage and the Dart Valley 1890 25965
We are on the upper reaches of the Dart, looking
north up the deeply incised valley towards the
tors of Dartmoor. On the right of the tall tree is
Mel Tor, and to the left is Bench Tor.

◆

HOLNE, THE CHURCH c1950 H101005
The 13th-century church of St Mary was enlarged in the 15th century. In 1819 Charles Kingsley, author of 'Westward Ho!' and 'The Water Babies', was born in the vicarage here while his father was curate in charge.

BUCKFASTLEIGH, THE VILLAGE c1965 B238051
Settled in the 13th century, and sited just downstream from the much older village of Buckfast, Buckfastleigh was for many years overshadowed by the nearby Stannary town of Ashburton. By the 19th century it was flourishing; it had five woollen mills and 700 looms, and the woollen trade lasted here later than anywhere else in the South Hams.

BUCKFASTLEIGH
The Bridge, Station Road c1960

The Dart was once a fine salmon river, and in 1933, just upstream from here, a Mr Donald caught the biggest salmon ever taken by rod and line on the river - a real monster that weighed in at 33 lb. The chimney in the background is that of the paper mill that operated here from 1785 to 1942.

TOTNES
Bridge Town 1890

In 1890 Bridge Town was the height of fashion, which accounts for all the smart town houses. The church of St John the Evangelist was built in 1835 by Edward Augustus Seymour, the 11th Duke of Somerset, who also built the Seymour Hotel, now converted to flats.

BUCKFASTLEIGH, THE BRIDGE, STATION ROAD c1960 B238017

TOTNES, BRIDGE TOWN 1890 25426

TOTNES, FORE STREET 1889 21628
On the skyline is the 120ft tower of St
Mary's, parish church of Totnes, built
in red sandstone by master mason
Roger Growdon and opened in 1450.
The interior was restored by Sir Giles
Gilbert Scott in 1862.

TOTNES, FORE STREET, LOOKING DOWN 1896 38222

TOTNES
Fore Street, Looking Down 1896
Fore Street remains little changed today, although the Paignton, Totnes and Torquay Omnibus Company has long since ceased to exist, and the fare is now considerably more than one shilling each way.

TOTNES
East Gate 1928
A gate has existed here since the 13th century; this arch dates from 1837, and the room above from the 16th century. On 4 September 1991 an electrical fault caused a disastrous fire which needed 15 fire appliances to get under control and caused £10 million of damage. The gate was restored and re-opened in 1992.

TOTNES, EAST GATE 1928 80998

TOTNES
The Landing Place and the Bridge 1896 38213
Totnes is at the upper limit of the tide, and it was here that the
lowest crossing of the Dart could be made, originally by ford and
later by bridge. The bridge, which replaced an older one built in
1692, was built in 1828 from local limestone by Charles Fowler, who
also designed Covent Garden. Today it is bypassed by
Brutus Bridge further upstream.

◆

TOTNES, THE LANDING PLACE AND THE BRIDGE 1896 38214

A popular leisure activity in Victorian times was to take a trip on the river by steamer: here we see it loading passengers from the Royal Seven Stars Hotel. Today, Steamer Quay is home to boatbuilders and chandlers, and in summer 2000 it saw the launch of Pete Goss's giant catamaran 'Team Phillips', the cause of many a red face when one of her revolutionary wave-piercing hulls broke off during sea-trials.

TOTNES, THE LANDING PLACE AND THE BRIDGE 1896 38214X

There is a lot of fun to be had while messing about on the river. Pulling skiffs such as these were a genteel way of getting fresh air and exercise, and their Thames equivalents inspired Jerome K Jerome's timeless 'Three Men in a Boat'. The gentleman at the foot of the slipway appears to be demonstrating his kayaking skills to a group of admiring ladies.

TOTNES, THE RIVER DART 1922 73223

The paddle steamer here is the 'Compton Castle'; this naming convention survives to this day on the South Devon coast, with pleasure boats called the 'Dartmouth Castle', the 'Salcombe Castle' and the 'Cardiff Castle'. Symons' Prize Medal Cyder was pressed until the 1940s on the Plains nearby, and, ironically, in the old Methodist Chapel, which still stands and has now been converted into flats.

BERRY POMEROY
The Castle Gateway 1890
Standing on a rock platform that was the home of the de la Pomerai family since Norman times, this medieval castle was built in the early 14th century on the site of an earlier manor.

BERRY POMEROY
The Castle, The Banqueting Hall 1928
The mansion was built inside the courtyard of the castle by Edward Seymour, Duke of Somerset, who bought Berry Pomeroy in 1548. Despite an outlay of £20,000, it was never quite completed; it later fell into disrepair. Apparently, opening the windows took a servant a whole day.

BERRY POMEROY, THE CASTLE GATEWAY 1890 25417

BERRY POMEROY, THE CASTLE, THE BANQUETING HALL 1928 81156

HARBERTONFORD, THE OLD ROAD c1965 H494012

The ford and bridge span the Harbourne River, a tributary of the Dart. The village was once known as Hernaford after a mansion built in 1285. The bridge was built in the late 16th or early 17th century.

HARBERTONFORD, GENERAL VIEW c1960 H494004

The large building was a woollen mill. These were once common throughout the South Hams, and towns such as Modbury, Buckfastleigh and Ivybridge grew wealthy from the fleeces of the sheep that grazed the rich pastures.

DARTMOUTH, ON THE DART 1889 21619
This is an idyllic spot on the banks of the Dart, and the scene remains unchanged. The little sailing boat is gunter-rigged, and slightly smaller than the gaff-rigged boat in picture 44587. Was it the same photographer ten years on trying to re-create the same scene?

DARTMOUTH, SHARPHAM BOATHOUSE 1899 44587

In the background is Sharpham House, built in 1770 by Captain Philemon Pownell on the site of an older house with gardens by Capability Brown. The good captain was spending the reward he received for capturing a Spanish ship, but unfortunately he never lived to see the house completed.

ASHPRINGTON, THE VILLAGE 1905 53221

At the time of the Domesday book in 1086, Ashprington was a valuable riverside estate, leased from the King by a wealthy Breton named Judhael, who held twenty manors in Devon alone. It had two salmon fisheries, and a salthouse used for salting meat and vegetables as well as the catch.

STOKE GABRIEL, THE CREEK c1965 S366010
Stoke Gabriel was for many years the centre of the Dart salmon fishery. From 15 March to 15 August salmon are netted as they run upstream to spawn, using a net rowed out from the shore to encircle the fish. Today there are few salmon fishermen left working.

STOKE GABRIEL, THE CHURCH HOUSE INN c1965 S366001
The Church House Inn, like many others of the same name in Devon, was probably built to house masons working on the construction of the church. Built in the 15th century (when ale was three farthings a gallon!) it was also used as a courthouse - the window on the far right is the room in question, handily situated above the stocks.

STOKE GABRIEL, THE YEW TREE c1965 S366023
The church of St Michael and St Gabriel has a 13th-century tower, and the body of the church dates from the 15th century - it was rebuilt after the original fell into disrepair in the 14th century. The yew tree in the churchyard, mentioned in the Domesday Book, is one of the biggest in the country and is at least 1,500 years old.

TOTNES, THE GREENWAY FERRY, THE RIVER DART 1924 76468
The ferry carries foot passengers to Dittisham. Greenway House was built by Sir Humphrey Gilbert, half-brother of Sir Walter Raleigh, and is reputed to be the place where a servant tried to extinguish his master with a bucket of water, thinking he was on fire when in fact he was enjoying a pipe of tobacco. It was also the home of Agatha Christie until her death in 1976.

MARLDON
The Village c1960
The church was built in the 15th and 16th centuries by the Gilberts of Compton Castle a mile away. Compton Castle, the best-fortified medieval manor in Devon, was built by Geoffrey Gilbert in 1326 and was restored in the 20th century by one of his descendants.

MARLDON
The Village c1960
The southern half of the parish has been absorbed into the urban sprawl of Torbay. It would be unrecognisable today to men like Sir John Gilbert, who claimed Newfoundland in 1583, or Raleigh Gilbert, one of the eight signatories to King James' charter in 1606 for the settling of America.

MARLDON, THE VILLAGE c1960 M168011

MARLDON, THE VILLAGE c1960 M168008

BATSON, THE CREEK 1895 35636

Judge Jeffreys held a court at Batson Hall during his bloody tour of the country after Monmouth's rebellion in 1685. The small building with the steeply-pitched roof on the right of the beach was the blacksmith's forge, and the house behind it was the inn.

KINGSWEAR, VIEW OF DARTMOUTH c1955 K34005

Seeing the river today, bustling with tourists and pleasure craft, it is difficult to imagine it playing a major role in history; but in 1147 the second crusade sailed from here, and in 1190 the third crusade, led by Richard I, also left the port. Later, Dartmouth was to send nine ships against the Armada.

DARTMOUTH, THE INNER HARBOUR c1955 D7104
Dartmouth's wealth came from its export of cloth from Totnes in the 13th and 14th centuries. John Hawley, a merchant and privateer who was mayor 14 times, was reputedly used as the model for the English sailor in the 'Canterbury Tales' by Geoffrey Chaucer after he visited Dartmouth in 1373.

DARTMOUTH, THE FERRY c1950 D7011
There has been a ferry at the lower crossing since Saxon times. The 19th-century horse ferry, rowed by two men with improbably long oars, charged a halfpenny per person or sheep and 2d for a horse. In 1877 the first steam tug was used to power the ferry, and the first car crossed in 1900.

DARTMOUTH, THE TOWN AND KINGSWEAR 1890 25275

Dartmouth's history has two great lost opportunities. In the 17th century it was considered as the site for a major naval base, but lost out to Plymouth; and in 1841 the Commission investigating the depot for the mail packet service recommended Dartmouth, but the service eventually went to Southampton.

DARTMOUTH, GENERAL VIEW 1918 68611

Standing on Mount Bourne in the background is the grand edifice of Britannia Royal Naval College, completed in 1905. The college was first established in 1863 aboard HMS Britannia in the river, and in 1872 the Prince of Wales sent his sons Albert and George to be educated there, starting a tradition carried on in the 20th century by Prince Charles and Prince Andrew.

KINGSWEAR, FROM DARTMOUTH 1890 25275X

The railway never reached Dartmouth itself, but it did come to Kingswear on the opposite shore in 1864. The quays and jetty were built in the hope of encouraging liners to dock, thereby knocking two days off the journey for passengers. The original broad gauge railway was narrowed to standard gauge by hundreds of men over a single weekend.

KINGSWEAR, GENERAL VIEW 1925 78366

By the 1930s the tourist trade was developing in both Dartmouth and Kingswear, and boarding houses and hotels were springing up. Large houses were maintained by richer visitors who came for the regatta, which often attracted royalty.

DARTMOUTH, THE 'MEW' 1918 68623
Ugly but efficient, and affectionately remembered, the 'Mew' carried passengers across the river from 1908 to 1954, and was converted to carry cars in the 1930s. She replaced the old paddle steamer 'Dolphin' which ran from 1869; she was pointed at both ends so that she could cross without having to turn round.

KINGSWEAR, GENERAL VIEW 1930 83084
Fifteen years after this picture was taken, the estuary presented a very different picture when it was crammed with 485 ships preparing for D-Day. They departed on 5 June 1945 for Utah beach on the Cotentin peninsula in Normandy.

KINGSWEAR, THE STATION c1955 K34002
The 'Mew' (alongside) had an adventurous life; in 1940 she was one of the fleet of 'little ships' who rescued the British Expeditionary Force from the beaches of Dunkirk, and on another occasion she helped rescue the French destroyer 'Mistral' when she was drifting helplessly in the estuary.

KINGSWEAR, GENERAL VIEW 1906 56628

The crane on the jetty was used for unloading coal, which was then taken by railway to Torquay gasworks. At one time 200 'coal lumpers' were employed, but the trade ceased in 1964 and the railway closed in 1969. Today the Dart Valley Railway operates a summer tourist service. Alongside is the old 'Dolphin'.

DARTMOUTH, BATTERY POINT 1889 21589

The tower visible here was built in 1488; it was a later addition to John Hawley's fort, which was started in the 1380s to deter Breton raiders. Godmerock, the fortress opposite, was built in 1502, and a chain was strung across the mouth of the river to secure the harbour.

Start Bay

START
The Lighthouse from the Ridge 1890 24539
Legend has it that locals watched the defeat of the Armada from here in 1588. The lighthouse was
built in 1834 and improved in the 1870s, and is visible from 21 miles away at sea.

TORCROSS
The Sands 1895 35640
Two miles south of here is the ghost village of Hallsands,
abandoned after it was destroyed in a storm in 1917. Twenty years
before, the Admiralty had started dredging 1,600 tons of shingle
daily from just offshore to make concrete for Devonport Dockyard.
Dredging stopped in 1902, but the shingle never returned, leaving
the village unprotected.

◆

TORCROSS, SLAPTON SANDS 1890 24543

Torcross itself has had a couple of brushes with oblivion; the most recent was in 1979, when it made the front pages after a violent storm which badly damaged the road and almost destroyed the village. A sea wall was built in 1980 to prevent a repetition.

TORCROSS, GENERAL VIEW 1925 78238

This is the inland part of Torcross, on the banks of Slapton Ley, a 270 acre fresh-water lake dammed by the shingle bank of 'the Line', as it is known. The Line is thought to be about 3,000 years old, and the Ley (in three parts - Upper Ley, Slapton Ley and Lower Ley) about 1,000 years old.

TORCROSS
THE SHORE 1930 83275
Torcross's fishermen kept Newfoundland dogs, which were trained to swim out and help tow the boats ashore in heavy weather. The boats were dragged up the beach on baulks of timber known as ways; their catch of crabs, for which the area was famous, was sent to London daily.

TORCROSS, GENERAL VIEW 1930 83271

Slapton Ley, fed by two streams, the Gara and the Start, is a fine fishing ground - in 1905 two men staying at the Torcross Hotel caught 21 pike and 1,812 perch and rudd (with rod and line, not nets!) during a four-day stay.

STOKENHAM, THE VILLAGE 1920 69842

In late 1943, 3,000 local residents had to leave their homes so that the US Army could practise their D-Day landings. Slapton Sands and its hinterland bore a striking resemblance to Utah Beach, and so homes and businesses were evacuated from Strete to Torcross and inland as far as Blackawton and East Allington farms.

STOKENHAM, THE CHURCH 1904 52466

The exercise was to be as realistic as possible, with live ammunition being used; despite the appeals of the Bishop of Exeter, Stokenham Church was badly damaged. The Church House Inn was shelled and mined, and to this day some buildings still have bullet holes.

SLAPTON, THE VILLAGE 1925 78244

Slapton is an ancient settlement, with an Iron Age fort. The Anglo-Saxon name was Sladona, meaning 'slippery place'. Thatching here is done with Slapton reed from the Ley, which has a reputation for durability.

SLAPTON, BOLD HILL 1925 78246

On the left is the ruined Chantry, founded in 1372 by Sir Guy de Bryan, Lord of the Manor of Slapton, and whose name is preserved in other South Hams settlements such as Torbryan. Four priests sang a service there every day until 1545.

SLAPTON, BROOK STREET 1925 78248

Slapton is now home to a field studies centre which runs courses for ecologists and biologists; they come to study the Ley, a Site of Special Scientific Interest and a National Nature Reserve, and home to an abundance of wildfowl, including the great crested grebe.

SLAPTON
The Ley and Start Bay 1930 83264
The Royal Sands Hotel, perched on the shingle bank of the Line,
was built in 1831. It came to a sad end just before D-Day when
Pincher Luscombe, a sheepdog, strayed through the barbed wire
surrounding it and set off a number of land mines,
completely destroying the hotel.

STRETE, THE TURNPIKE 1925 78262

STRETE, THE UNITED STATES ARMY MEMORIAL c1955 S223006

STRETE
The Turnpike 1925
Strete stands high on a hill above Start Bay; its 500 or so inhabitants live in houses built from Dartmouth slate. In 1864 the old packhorse track from Strete to Torcross was made into a turnpike road - these cottages stand at the Strete end.

STRETE
The United States Army Memorial c1955
The memorial, presented by the USA and unveiled in 1954, commemorates the 1,000 men who died during Operation Tiger, the rehearsal for the D-Day landings. 700 died when German E-boats sank three landing craft, and another 300 died when supporting naval vessels laid their artillery barrage too low.

BLACKPOOL, THE SANDS 1925 78361

Blackpool's golden shingle beach and wooded hills have an almost Mediterranean air about them, and they are often used as a location for films. One location scout decided they looked like the South American coast; the beach ended up being the backdrop for ITV's film about Francis Drake, starring John Thaw.

BLACKPOOL, THE BRIDGE 1918 68248

This is a sleepy little place, but one which has had its fair share of excitement. In 1404 a force led by the Breton William du Chatel comprising 300 ships and 2,000 knights landed here to attack Dartmouth, but were defeated by a force that included women and children. A Te Deum was sung in Westminster Abbey to celebrate.

BLACKPOOL, THE COTTAGES c1960 B117026

In 1470 Warwick the Kingmaker fled to France via Dartmouth after failing to overthrow Edward IV. On his return, he landed at Blackpool before travelling north to complete his unseating of the king.

BLACKPOOL, THE VILLAGE 1918 68247

Blackpool's woodlands once extended much further seaward; in 1869 a storm revealed tree stumps in the clay beneath the beach. This old forest was submerged by the formation of the Line 1,000 years ago.

STOKE FLEMING, THE CHURCH AND THE VILLAGE 1925 78385

STOKE FLEMING
The Church and the Village 1925
The 13th-century tower of the church of St Peter, on top of a hill, is a prominent landmark; it was once used as a marker by ships entering the Dart. The 14th-century brass of John and Elinor Corp is the oldest to be found in any South Hams church.

◆

STOKE FLEMING
The Village 1934
A famous rector of St Peter's was Elias Newcomen, great-grandfather of Thomas, inventor of the steam engine. Elias was over 80 when he was expelled from his church after the Civil War, but he lived to see the Restoration of the monarchy and returned to Stoke Fleming aged over 100.

STOKE FLEMING, THE VILLAGE 1934 86230

STOKE FLEMING, MAIN STREET 1934 86232

STOKE FLEMING
Main Street 1934
One of the village's most famous former residents - he bought a house here, and is buried in the churchyard - was the 'Calculating Boy' George Parker Bidder. Having entertained Queen Victoria with his mental abilities, he grew up to become an engineer, working with George Stephenson on railways and building Victoria Docks in London.

◆

STOKE FLEMING
The Caravan Site c1960
This photograph shows a rather different form of living from that described in the Domesday Book, when Stoke Fleming was a rich manor and bigger than nearby Dartmouth. It boasted a watermill, three carthorses, 16 cattle, five pigs, 260 sheep and 25 villagers.

STOKE FLEMING, THE CARAVAN SITE c1960 S200017

Index

Frith Book Co Titles

www.frithbook.co.uk

The Frith Book Company publishes over 100 new titles each year. A selection of those currently available are listed below. For latest catalogue please contact Frith Book Co.

Town Books 96pp, 100 photos. County and Themed Books 128pp, 150 photos (unless specified). All titles hardback laminated case and jacket except those indicated pb (paperback)

Around Bakewell	1-85937-113-2	£12.99	Around Great Yarmouth	1-85937-085-3	£12.99
Around Barnstaple	1-85937-084-5	£12.99	Around Guildford	1-85937-117-5	£12.99
Around Bath	1-85937-097-7	£12.99	Hampshire	1-85937-064-0	£14.99
Berkshire (pb)	1-85937-191-4	£9.99	Around Harrogate	1-85937-112-4	£12.99
Around Blackpool	1-85937-049-7	£12.99	Around Horsham	1-85937-127-2	£12.99
Around Bognor Regis	1-85937-055-1	£12.99	Around Ipswich	1-85937-133-7	£12.99
Around Bournemouth	1-85937-067-5	£12.99	Ireland (pb)	1-85937-181-7	£9.99
Brighton (pb)	1-85937-192-2	£8.99	Isle of Man	1-85937-065-9	£14.99
British Life A Century Ago	1-85937-103-5	£17.99	Isle of Wight	1-85937-114-0	£14.99
Buckinghamshire (pb)	1-85937-200-7	£9.99	Kent (pb)	1-85937-189-2	£9.99
Around Cambridge	1-85937-092-6	£12.99	Around Leicester	1-85937-073-x	£12.99
Cambridgeshire	1-85937-086-1	£14.99	Leicestershire (pb)	1-85937-185-x	£9.99
Canals and Waterways	1-85937-129-9	£17.99	Around Lincoln	1-85937-111-6	£12.99
Cheshire	1-85937-045-4	£14.99	Lincolnshire	1-85937-135-3	£14.99
Around Chester	1-85937-090-x	£12.99	London (pb)	1-85937-183-3	£9.99
Around Chichester	1-85937-089-6	£12.99	Around Maidstone	1-85937-056-x	£12.99
Churches of Berkshire	1-85937-170-1	£17.99	New Forest	1-85937-128-0	£14.99
Churches of Dorset	1-85937-172-8	£17.99	Around Newark	1-85937-105-1	£12.99
Colchester (pb)	1-85937-188-4	£8.99	Around Newquay	1-85937-140-x	£12.99
Cornwall	1-85937-054-3	£14.99	North Devon Coast	1-85937-146-9	£14.99
Cumbria	1-85937-101-9	£14.99	Northumberland and Tyne & Wear		
Dartmoor	1-85937-145-0	£14.99		1-85937-072-1	£14.99
Around Derby	1-85937-046-2	£12.99	Norwich (pb)	1-85937-194-9	£8.99
Derbyshire (pb)	1-85937-196-5	£9.99	Around Nottingham	1-85937-060-8	£12.99
Devon	1-85937-052-7	£14.99	Nottinghamshire (pb)	1-85937-187-6	£9.99
Dorset	1-85937-075-6	£14.99	Around Oxford	1-85937-096-9	£12.99
Dorset Coast	1-85937-062-4	£14.99	Oxfordshire	1-85937-076-4	£14.99
Down the Severn	1-85937-118-3	£14.99	Peak District	1-85937-100-0	£14.99
Down the Thames	1-85937-121-3	£14.99	Around Penzance	1-85937-069-1	£12.99
Around Dublin	1-85937-058-6	£12.99	Around Plymouth	1-85937-119-1	£12.99
East Sussex	1-85937-130-2	£14.99	Around St Ives	1-85937-068-3	£12.99
Around Eastbourne	1-85937-061-6	£12.99	Around Scarborough	1-85937-104-3	£12.99
Edinburgh (pb)	1-85937-193-0	£8.99	Scotland (pb)	1-85937-182-5	£9.99
English Castles	1-85937-078-0	£14.99	Scottish Castles	1-85937-077-2	£14.99
Essex	1-85937-082-9	£14.99	Around Sevenoaks and Tonbridge		
Around Exeter	1-85937-126-4	£12.99		1-85937-057-8	£12.99
Exmoor	1-85937-132-9	£14.99	Around Southampton	1-85937-088-8	£12.99
Around Falmouth	1-85937-066-7	£12.99	Around Southport	1-85937-106-x	£12.99

Available from your local bookshop or from the publisher

Frith Book Co Titles (continued)

Around Shrewsbury	1-85937-110-8	£12.99
Shropshire	1-85937-083-7	£14.99
South Devon Coast	1-85937-107-8	£14.99
South Devon Living Memories		
	1-85937-168-x	£14.99
Staffordshire (96pp)	1-85937-047-0	£12.99
Stone Circles & Ancient Monuments		
	1-85937-143-4	£17.99
Around Stratford upon Avon		
	1-85937-098-5	£12.99
Sussex (pb)	1-85937-184-1	£9.99

Around Torbay	1-85937-063-2	£12.99
Around Truro	1-85937-147-7	£12.99
Victorian & Edwardian Kent		
	1-85937-149-3	£14.99
Victorian & Edwardian Yorkshire		
	1-85937-154-x	£14.99
Warwickshire (pb)	1-85937-203-1	£9.99
Welsh Castles	1-85937-120-5	£14.99
West Midlands	1-85937-109-4	£14.99
West Sussex	1-85937-148-5	£14.99
Wiltshire	1-85937-053-5	£14.99
Around Winchester	1-85937-139-6	£12.99

Frith Book Co titles available Autumn 2000

Croydon Living Memories (pb)			
	1-85937-162-0	£9.99	Aug
Glasgow (pb)	1-85937-190-6	£9.99	Aug
Hertfordshire (pb)	1-85937-247-3	£9.99	Aug
North London	1-85937-206-6	£14.99	Aug
Victorian & Edwardian Maritime Album			
	1-85937-144-2	£17.99	Aug
Victorian Seaside	1-85937-159-0	£17.99	Aug
Cornish Coast	1-85937-163-9	£14.99	Sep
County Durham	1-85937-123-x	£14.99	Sep
Dorset Living Memories	1-85937-210-4	£14.99	Sep
Herefordshire	1-85937-174-4	£14.99	Sep
Kent Living Memories	1-85937-125-6	£14.99	Sep
Leeds (pb)	1-85937-202-3	£9.99	Sep
Ludlow (pb)	1-85937-176-0	£9.99	Sep
Norfolk (pb)	1-85937-195-7	£9.99	Sep
Somerset	1-85937-153-1	£14.99	Sep
Tees Valley & Cleveland	1-85937-211-2	£14.99	Sep
Thanet (pb)	1-85937-116-7	£9.99	Sep
Tiverton (pb)	1-85937-178-7	£9.99	Sep
Victorian and Edwardian Sussex			
	1-85937-157-4	£14.99	Sep

Weymouth (pb)	1-85937-209-0	£9.99	Sep
Worcestershire	1-85937-152-3	£14.99	Sep
Yorkshire Living Memories	1-85937-166-3	£14.99	Sep
British Life A Century Ago (pb)			
	1-85937-213-9	£9.99	Oct
Camberley (pb)	1-85937-222-8	£9.99	Oct
Cardiff (pb)	1-85937-093-4	£9.99	Oct
Carmarthenshire	1-85937-216-3	£14.99	Oct
Cornwall (pb)	1-85937-229-5	£9.99	Oct
English Country Houses	1-85937-161-2	£17.99	Oct
Humberside	1-85937-215-5	£14.99	Oct
Manchester (pb)	1-85937-198-1	£9.99	Oct
Middlesex	1-85937-158-2	£14.99	Oct
Norfolk Living Memories	1-85937-217-1	£14.99	Oct
Preston (pb)	1-85937-212-0	£9.99	Oct
South Hams	1-85937-220-1	£14.99	Oct
Suffolk	1-85937-221-x	£9.99	Oct
Swansea (pb)	1-85937-167-1	£9.99	Oct
West Yorkshire (pb)	1-85937-201-5	£9.99	Oct

See Frith books on the internet www.frithbook.co.uk

FRITH PRODUCTS & SERVICES

Francis Frith would doubtless be pleased to know that the pioneering publishing venture he started in 1860 still continues today. A hundred and forty years later, The Francis Frith Collection continues in the same innovative tradition and is now one of the foremost publishers of vintage photographs in the world. Some of the current activities include:

Interior Decoration

Today Frith's photographs can be seen framed and as giant wall murals in thousands of pubs, restaurants, hotels, banks, retail stores and other public buildings throughout the country. In every case they enhance the unique local atmosphere of the places they depict and provide reminders of gentler days in an increasingly busy and frenetic world.

Product Promotions

Frith products are used by many major companies to promote the sales of their own products or to reinforce their own history and heritage. Frith promotions have been used by Hovis bread, Courage beers, Scots Porage Oats, Colman's mustard, Cadbury's foods, Mellow Birds coffee, Dunhill pipe tobacco, Guinness, and Bulmer's Cider.

Genealogy and Family History

As the interest in family history and roots grows world-wide, more and more people are turning to Frith's photographs of Great Britain for images of the towns, villages and streets where their ancestors lived; and, of course, photographs of the churches and chapels where their ancestors were christened, married and buried are an essential part of every genealogy tree and family album.

Frith Products

All Frith photographs are available Framed or just as Mounted Prints and Posters (size 23 x 16 inches). These may be ordered from the address below. From time to time other products - Address Books, Calendars, Table Mats, etc - are available.

The Internet

Already twenty thousand Frith photographs can be viewed and purchased on the internet. By the end of the year 2000 some 60,000 Frith photographs will be available on the internet. The number of sites is constantly expanding, each focussing on different products and services from the Collection.
The main Frith sites are listed below.
www.francisfrith.co.uk
www.frithbook.co.uk

See the complete list of Frith Books at:
www.frithbook.co.uk
This web site is regularly updated with the latest list of publications from the Frith Book Company. If you wish to buy books relating to another part of the country that your local bookshop does not stock, you may purchase on-line.

For further information, trade, or author enquiries please contact us at the address below:
The Francis Frith Collection, Frith's Barn, Teffont, Salisbury, Wiltshire, England SP3 5QP.
Tel: +44 (0)1722 716 376 Fax: +44 (0)1722 716 881 Email: uksales@francisfrith.com

See Frith books on the internet www.frithbook.co.uk

TO RECEIVE YOUR FREE MOUNTED PRINT

Mounted Print
Overall size 14 x 11 inches

Cut out this Voucher and return it with your remittance for £1.50 to cover postage and handling, to UK addresses. For overseas addresses please include £4.00 post and handling. Choose any photograph included in this book. Your SEPIA print will be A4 in size, and mounted in a cream mount with burgundy rule lines, overall size 14 x 11 inches.

Order additional Mounted Prints at HALF PRICE (only £7.49 each*)

If there are further pictures you would like to order, possibly as gifts for friends and family, purchase them at half price (no additional postage and handling required).

Have your Mounted Prints framed*

For an additional £14.95 per print you can have your chosen Mounted Print framed in an elegant polished wood and gilt moulding, overall size 16 x 13 inches (no additional postage and handling required).

---

* IMPORTANT!
These special prices are only available if ordered using the original voucher on this page (no copies permitted) and at the same time as your free Mounted Print, for delivery to the same address

---

Frith Collectors' Guild

From time to time we publish a magazine of news and stories about Frith photographs and further special offers of Frith products. If you would like 12 months FREE membership, please return this form.

Send completed forms to:
The Francis Frith Collection, Frith's Barn, Teffont, Salisbury, Wiltshire SP3 5QP

Voucher for FREE and Reduced Price Frith Prints

Picture no.	Page number	Qty	Mounted @ £7.49	Framed + £14.95	Total Cost
		1	**Free of charge***	£	£
			£7.49	£	£
			£7.49	£	£
			£7.49	£	£
			£7.49	£	£
			£7.49	£	£

Please allow 28 days for delivery	*** Post & handling**	**£1.50**
Book Title	**Total Order Cost**	**£**

Please do not photocopy this voucher. Only the original is valid, so please cut it out and return it to us.

I enclose a cheque / postal order for £ . . . .
made payable to 'The Francis Frith Collection'
OR please debit my Mastercard / Visa / Switch / Amex card

Number . . . .

Issue No (Switch only) . . . . .Valid from (Amex/Switch) . . . .

Expires . . . . Signature . . . .

Name Mr/Mrs/Ms . . . .

Address . . . .

. . . .

. . . .

. . . . Postcode . . . .

Daytime Tel No . . . .   Valid to 31/12/02

The Francis Frith Collectors' Guild

Please enrol me as a member for 12 months free of charge.

Name Mr/Mrs/Ms . . . .

Address . . . .

. . . .

. . . .

. . . . Postcode . . . .

Free Print - see overleaf